Friendly Univers

heart2heart

Be Yourself —
Everyone Else Is Taken

He drew a circle that shut me out
Heretic, rebel, a thing to flout
But love and I had the wit to win:
We drew a circle that took him in.

— Edwin Markham

Ardys U. Reverman, Ph.D.

Illustrated by Charlotte Lewis

1993-#1-All About You in the Creative Circle
1999-#2-Newly Revised and Expanded Edition TeamSmart SQ
2006 Library of Congress Cataloging in Publication Data
Reverman, Ardys U.

heart2heart: Be Yourself — Everyone Else Is Taken
Summary: Partnership is an adventure into who you are and what you care about, a new way of whole-brain learning. You learn about the way you think and how your point of view fits with everyone you meet.
p. 223 cm.
1. Self-respect. 2. Self-perception. 3. Success—Psychological aspects.
4. Personality development. 5. Temperament strengths.
6. Parental acceptance. 7. Cognition I Title. 8. Collaboration
BF697.5.S54.R   1999
158.1   20   98-060225
                       CIP

ISBN 978-0-9625385-6-8

Visit us on the web at
www.synergypals.com
www.friendlyuniverse.com

Think   Look   Talk   Feel

This Book Belongs To

_____

Color Me SENSE-sational!

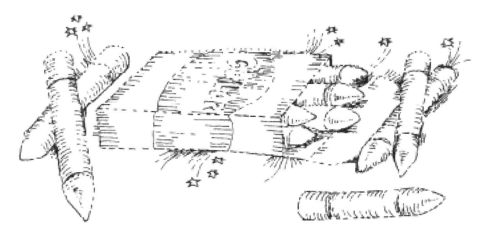

I'll Fly Away

_In loving memory of
my kith and kin who
in living made full use of
their gifts, reminders of
the power and beauty
of differences._

Contents

*There are only two or three human stories,
and they go on repeating themselves as fiercely
as if they had never happened before.*

Willa Cather

Foreword

It is difficult to put emotions and feelings into words, not just for children, but for mature, wise adults. There is no doubt that we could learn better skills to communicate with our children and each other. While animals smell each other, humans guess another's emotions by what is shown on the face: anger, love, boredom, anxiety, fear, pain, etc. We can do the Haim Ginott strategy of "I see you are angry. Can you tell me about it?" But who remembers what to ask when one is tired or distracted? The meaning of the communication is the response it elicits, because language affects the nervous system.

Opposites attract, then they attack, yet it isn't meant to be that way. We discover how we are designed to be each other's best teacher in order to understand our own subjectivity. Synergy puts another spin on the ball of perception. Reconciliation propels us to evolve. That's why making up feels so good. Our brain connections attract more connections for more meaningful choices. Knowledge is an active verb of love and shared power.

We also know that people are different; some are hyper, some are calm and collected, some learn by doing, some learn by hearing or feeling or reading. We are all different. Dr. Reverman has captured those differences in this work and made it easy and natural for child and adult to get back into the communication and understanding mode so that everyone in the family can be comfortable and accepted. Once that has happened, children develop good self-images. This is the chief purpose for childhood—to achieve a positive self-concept so that when that child matures, he or she will be a contributing, fulfilled adult. Parents have given their children a good self-image, which is the chief job for childhood.

— *the late Lendon H. Smith, M.D.*

(Lendon Smith was the most recognized "children's doctor" in the nation, and author of many books, including *Hyper Kids, Improving Your Child's Behavior Chemistry, How to Raise a Healthy Child—Medical and Nutritional Advice from America's Best-Loved Pediatrician*)

*A human being is a part of the whole,
called by us "Universe," a part limited in
time and space. He experiences himself,
his thoughts and feelings as something
separated from the rest—a kind of
optical illusion of his consciousness.
This delusion is a kind of prison for us,
restricting us to our personal desire and
to affection for a few persons nearest us.
Our task must be to free ourselves from this
prison by widening our circle of compassion
to embrace all living creatures and the
whole of nature in its beauty.
Nobody is able to achieve this completely,
but the striving for such achievement is itself
a part of the liberation and foundation
for inner security.*

Albert Einstein

Friendly Universe Collection #1

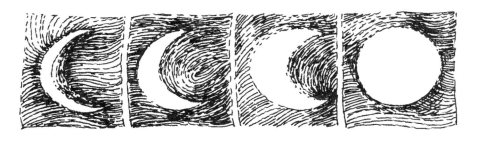

Messages for Adults

Learning Together with the Synergy Pals

The Synergy Pals takes you (parent, grandparent, family member, educator—any caring adult) on an interactive journey of self-discovery with your child. This book is meant to be read aloud and shared together, as partners. After you learn how easy it is to recognize the various personalities (the Synergy Pals), you will be able to unite the tensions of opposite styles into a positive, compatible synergy— a way to work and play smarter together. Knowledge is an active verb of love and shared power.

Encourage your child to color the pictures in the book. The four colors green, red, yellow, and blue have special meanings here, each representing one of four personality characters of the Synergy Pals. Each Pal has a special style of learning, living and feeling: There's the step-by-step thinking process of Thinkabout Owl (represented by green), the hands-on practice of Feelabout Koala (red), the inventive ideas of Talkabout Chimp (yellow), and the back-from-the-future visions of Lookabout Lion (blue). Together, they form a co-creative team.

A Child's Personality Development

Though you and your child may be of different personality (or temperament) types, it is the fit, not the type, that determines the course of the child's development. We all need to learn what we are good at and how we fit in. Then we can successfully develop our own natural gifts for self-fulfillment and make the most of our relationships with others.

Understanding our own personality style begins with understanding how we all learn and grow. Brain/mind research tells us that we learn more and retain more of what we learn when we are alert, relaxed, and feeling safe. When we approach change naturally and with pleasure, we have far better results in terms of both our intrapersonal intelligence (knowing who we are) and our interpersonal intelligence (learning from and helping each other).

Our thoughts generate desires, motives, and values; these are felt and expressed as needs, which lead us to act. If our own personality remains unknown or unacknowledged, and our needs unmet, we may live as an enigma inside and out, flip-flopping between isolation and clinging dependency. This instability can lock us into a lifetime of inappropriate behavior. Though a true personality style may be masked for years, ultimately it will manifest itself.

If we, consciously or unconsciously, become too polarized by our own personality type, we lose the freedom to choose to act differently. Then it becomes easy for us to spend a lifetime seeking and conflicting with our polar opposites.

As everything does the rate of growth and change will accelerate to interact with a diverse global network. Survival of the wittiest brings this information at a time we are aware patterns endure in human behavior. Love needs to motivate us and tap into universal knowledge. Over the years temperaments have been called by many names. I prefer sensory based think, look, talk, feel to get at the talents as well as the core values of the sensory pattern it identifies, and works for everyone in all cultures.

Consider how people are so often attracted to their opposite personality type—the orderly with the spontaneous, the agreeable with the controlling, the reflective with the expressive, the exacting with the generalizing. The tensions of opposites co-create and co-evolve us. Our natural desire to interact with others, including the wish to help our children, is frequently misunderstood and rejected when personality types are mismatched. This may result in arguments, withdrawal, and alienation. Technically, we may be saying all of the right words, but we still need to understand how to satisfy the needs of others' hearts by learning to speak each other's emotional language. This language comes from one's own particular personality and determines how each of us interprets and interacts with the world around us. We create a good learning fit.

Brain research is robust and shows that much of who we are is determined by boy and girl brain differences: the on/off switch of multi-tasking and talking for girls and the focus skills of the hunt for boys. Hormones and socializing influences can channel this boy and girl biology into life's creative forces. Given the right drive, skill, and nurturing, boys and girls can succeed in their own ways of doing things. Boys like clear winners and losers and personal achievement. Girls like relationships and play inclusive games like school or store. Excluding a BFF can be a devastating punishment and is part of a woman's relational role all their lives—we are designed to evolve—protecting each other, with inclusivity for all. By living kinship we reach beyond self from cradle to grave. The more we understand how we and others think, learn, and interrelate, the more we can contribute to the intellectual and emotional development of our children and to our healthy, joyful relationships with them.

Synergy puts another spin on the ball of perception. By understanding these differences, by encouraging the development of each one's unique ways of dealing with the world, and by guiding them into appropriate channels, we set the stage for powerful results. We are able to work *with* each other rather than fighting against, and that positive energy becomes synergy. Working together we achieve far more than working apart.

The Shared Power of Synergy

As Alfred Korzybski reminds us, "The map [our experience] is not the territory [the world]." Each of us perceives a different and equally real reality. We see things as we are, not as they are. Ideally, we use our interactions with the world to explore our reality, to question it, to stretch its boundaries, thereby moving the whole circle of learning back to our true selves.

Our mind either locks us into a limited "flat" worldview or hurdles us over the fear of the unknown so we can stretch beyond our own viewpoint. Then we can incorporate new possibilities by embracing how we all learn, individually and collectively.

Einstein's theory of relativity has helped us to see the benefits of a totally connected universe. We can interact powerfully within this natural framework by forming chains of awareness. Understanding links us with other people so we all have access to each other's talents. This co-creative view of synergy may sound complicated, but it's easy to see how it works when you and your child start playing along with the Synergy Pals. heart2heart. Be – Love – Do: Be who you are... Love everything...Do what your talents dictate.

The things we love to do and the things we are good at come together as the world evolves. The very future of our communities and institutions depend on it. The world is changing faster than ever in our history. Our best hope for the future is to develop a new paradigm of human capacity to meet a new era of human existence. We need to evolve a new appreciation of the importance of nurturing human talent long with an understanding of how talent expresses itself differently in every individual— where every person is inspired to grow creatively.

— Ken Robinson, Ph.D.
The Element: How Finding Your Passion Changes Everything

Thinkabout Owl, Lookabout Lion,
Talkabout Chimp, and Feelabout Koala
learn how to stay healthy and have fun
through all of the work and the play,
one and all, every day.
For each is a part of the Whole.

Thinkabout Owl, Lookabout Lion,
Talkabout Chimp, and Feelabout Koala
all name their troubles and tell themselves,
Now I'll learn from the rest
and still be my best for
I am a part of the Whole.

SENSE-sational Synergy Pals

I am the Talkabout Chimp: I need ideas and I love understanding. My imagination just flies. I don't know where I'm landing. If I feel misunderstood, I can even get rude. When ignored, I'll go into a mood. I value our talk, its inspiring you know. Routine makes me noisy with fright. Organization is so depressing and slow that I'll soon be clear out of sight.

I am the Thinkabout Owl: I need facts, then I put them in order. I stand them in rows or I give them a border. I feel a bit cornered when you push me toward a goal or criticize while I move slowly forward. I value the time to think in my head. I'll not move too fast 'til I'm right. I'll gather more facts and more facts, instead of jumping and taking a flight.

I am the Lookabout Lion: I need challenge and ultimate freedom to plan, to do, to get through, when I see some goal in my mind. If you won't decide, you don't take the ride. I feel blocked, like you're not at my side. I value results, the good things that goal brings. I can push 'til I get my own way. I'll get serious and bossy about just one thing. Act like you have no feelings and nothing to say.

I am the Feelabout Koala: I need love and a nice harmony. I'll share and I'll play. I'll help you each day — and feel good about it, if I am not left out. You must care how I feel, or I'll pout or I'll shout. I value my feelings, my friends, being happy. I'll always say "yes" to please you. I'll squash myself down if you get too snappy. It hurts my insides when you do.

If you could look inside your thoughts through a magic window, what do you suppose you'd see?

You'd see the different parts of your personality, everything that makes you who you are—the values, beliefs, and feelings that affect your thinking and behavior. You'd discover what you really want and how satisfied you'll feel when you see you're a whole person with a mind and hidden talents of your own. How happy you'd be with this vision!

The magic window is like
a prism with four colors
showing the thinking lights inside.

Think   Look   Talk   Feel

We're going to show you a special magic window—one that will help you see inside of you. When you look through it, you'll see animals with colors green, blue, yellow, and red, one for each of your own points of view— Think, Look, Talk, and Feel.

♡ These animals show you different ways that people look at the world.

♡ You see things based on what you are already thinking. Your thoughts tell you what to see—and what not to see.

♡ The animals are just another way of looking at the different parts inside of YOU, and others, too. You'll see a little bit of yourself in each one of the four animals.

♡ As you learn more about them, your heart may tell you that one of the four is more like YOU than the others and more special to you. Which one is most like YOU? Ask your heart and then imagine…what were you born to do best?

The magic window reveals
the natural talents inside of you.

The SENSE-sational

Imagine your senses seeing things from the four points of view of the Synergy Pals, as a...

Thinkabout Owl,

Lookabout Lion,

Talkabout Chimp,

Feelabout Koala.

Which one is most like YOU right now? At different times, you'll see that each Synergy Pal is a think, look, talk, or feel sense inside you. You also learn to stretch and "meet" the Synergy Pal least like you. The match or mismatch of these senses is what counts.

Something we were withholding
made us weak
Until we found it was ourselves.

Robert Frost

We dance 'round the ring and suppose,
but the secret sits in the middle and knows.

Robert Frost

Talkabout Chimp
Inspires
Ideas

Talkabout Chimp

When I'm a Talkabout Chimp

If I were a Chimp, a Talkabout Chimp,
ideas would whirl through my mind.
They'd dance 'til I'm crazy and
twirl 'til I'm dizzy,
until I can barely unwind.

I'm good at pretending,
expressing, inventing,
I'm artist and actor at play.
I'm often creative
and so innovative,
I do many things in new ways.

I like to be out
with nature about.
There's so much to
hear 'neath the sky.
A talk with my friend
is the very best way
to catch the ideas that fly by.

I love to talk to friends about ideas,
and I have so very many questions.

I crave understanding,
I can be demanding,
my wishes not easily met.
With your indecision,
mocking or meanness,
I'll frown and I'll fidget and fret.

If you reject me, it hurts.
Ignoring's the worst
kind of treatment
I'll ever endure.
Then I put things off,
withdraw, become moody,
feeling very unsure.

I love it when I can
do something new and different.

I love to question the rules
and the reasons
and do what seems right to me.
I need your affection and
true understanding
to feel that I really am free.

So, give me a hand;
please listen and lend
your thoughts to the
projects I've planned.
For I need to know
that I can be friends
with someone who does understand.

When I have fun with friends
putting on a show, I feel great!

Talkabout Chimp

When I'm a Talkabout kind of person,
I need to feel understood,
to share my ideas and be creative.

I like to... *(check the boxes most like you)*

☐ hear people explain how to do something.

☐ choose what I want to learn.

☐ shout with joy.

☐ find different ways to do an assignment.

☐ hear people talking in soft, nice voices all around me.

☐ talk to myself while I do a problem or task.

- [ ] talk about what scares me or makes me angry or happy.

- [ ] talk in a loud or quiet voice, whichever sounds best to me.

- [ ] hear about legends and myths and what other people believe.

- [ ] talk while everyone listens to my ideas.

- [ ] share my ideas first, and see how others react.

- [ ] play games that use my ideas and imagination.

- [ ] do lots of different things at the same time.

- [ ] be in plays, where I can express myself.

Talkabout You

Who listens to and understands **me**?

What questions are on **my** mind today?

If **I** were going to do a show, what kind of show would it be?

Am I someone who likes to share ideas, listen and talk, have hunches in bunches and be the one who loves to have fun?

Through my Talkabout window, I share inspired ideas and dreams. I know how to understand others and be understood.

Am I a Talkabout Chimp who likes to listen and talk about ideas and have understanding?

I know but one freedom, and that is the freedom of the mind.

Antoine de Saint Exupery

Thinkabout
Owl
Practices
Carefully

Thinkabout Owl

When I'm a Thinkabout Owl

If I were an Owl, a Thinkabout Owl,
you'd find me alone in my room,
enjoying the quiet, enjoying my thoughts,
so don't interrupt me too soon.

Oh, I love to ponder
the meaning and wonder,
the workings of this and of that…
the order of numbers
and patterns and rhythms
of systems and logic and maps.

I like my room neat
and it's really a treat
for me to arrange it my way,
so don't wait around
for a finishing sound,
I just might be busy all day.

I'd be amazed to see on paper
all the figurings and feelings
going through my mind in just one day.

I need things in order,
a predictable future
with everything tidy and straight.
If things get too messy
or plans get too iffy,
how can I expect to create?

When I am aware of
confusion and scared,
I freeze,
and don't know what I should do.
Then I may get
stubborn, unfriendly, aloof,
and even
stop talking to you.

It's okay for me to like details and
want things in order.

Now please understand
that I do need a friend,
and my feelings don't know what to say.
You'll just have to know
that I like you although
I seem to be running away.

I really like facts, with
step-by-step lessons.
I'll do the best work that I can.
So, tell me exactly
what you expect,
and I'll produce the ideas you plan.

Just give me some time
for being alone,
to put my surroundings to mend.
Then I'll be ready
for more conversations
and riddles and games with my friend.

When I feel safe, it's easy for me
to work and have fun with others,
even very different types of people.

Thinkabout Owl

When I'm a Thinkabout kind of person,
I need to know everything is in order,
safe, and correct!

I like to... *(check the boxes most like you)*

☐ take my time before I act on an idea.

☐ use skills I already have.

☐ explain ideas step by step.

☐ earn my own spending money.

☐ read about how things are discovered and the reasons
why they are special.

- [ ] control my own things and have a special place where I make the rules.

- [ ] know exactly what to do.

- [ ] have all my things lined up in order.

- [ ] not have to tell others how I really feel if I'm upset.

- [ ] be on time and have my friends be on time to meet me.

- [ ] be loyal to my friends and take good care of my pets.

Thinkabout You

Whom do **I** feel safe with and like to do things with?

What's going through **my** mind today?

What sort of things do **I** most like to keep in order?

thinkabout owl

Am I someone who likes to sit in my room where I feel safe as I quietly think and work by myself? Do I like to figure things out carefully and put everything in order?

Through my Thinkabout window, I know how to gather details and plans and keep order and safety.

Am I a Thinkabout Owl who likes to be safe at home and have things in order and time to think?

Birds
build their nests
in circles,
for theirs is
the same religion
as ours.

Black Elk

Lookabout
Lion
Leads Tomorrow

Lookabout
Lion

When I'm a Lookabout Lion

If I were a Lion, a Lookabout Lion,
the world would be mine to explore.
I'd be a leader or clever inventor
of what's never been tried before.

My plans are so huge,
so tall and so wide
they go way out into space.
I wish to move forward
and upward and onward
and follow my vision someplace.

I'm a person of action.
I see the attraction
of having control of my fate.
I like to take charge
of projects so large,
and, with others, accomplish the great.

I know I can build wonderful things —
houses, boats, and giant rockets
to explore outer space.

So don't get in my way
or make me delay
the task I have set for myself.
For I must be free
to do wondrous deeds —
not tied up or put on the shelf.

And if I feel caged,
I'll roar and I'll rage,
I'll yell, I'll demand, and I'll snap.
I'll quickly take action
in any direction
that might get me out of a trap.

I'm brave and always ready to explore.
I can see in my mind a plan that will get things done.

I always need freedom
and room to move on.
I hate things that get in my way.
You may feel amazed,
confronted, and dazed
or hurt by the things that I say.

Please understand,
that's the way that I am,
it's the way I try to break free.
Don't cower or cringe
if your feelings get singed,
just stand up and tell it to me.

I feel good when everyone cooperates
to do one of my projects,
and I feel proud when I can take charge
to make sure the job is done well.

Lookabout Lion

When I'm a Lookabout kind of person,
I need to feel free, have choices,
and get results!

I like to... *(check the boxes most like you)*

☐ imagine what life will be like in the future.

☐ choose by myself the direction I want to go.

☐ search for solutions to problems.

☐ work on something that takes a long time.

☐ have a quiet place where I can think.

☐ watch others work while they explain to me what they're doing.

- [ ] choose clothes in my favorite colors that make me look good.

- [ ] look at pictures in books and read stories that explain the how and why of things.

- [ ] draw diagrams to explain my ideas.

- [ ] see by people's smiling faces that they like me.

- [ ] have lots of pencils, colored markers, and big sheets of clean paper for my use.

- [ ] talk or listen only when I want to.

- [ ] have the colors and things around me look nice and neat.

- [ ] go to museums or other interesting places and explore them for as long as I want.

Lookabout You

What would **I** invent and what places would **I** explore?

What plans or projects do **I** have right now?

What projects have I done well with others?

Am I someone who likes to have choices and wants to make quick decisions? Am I able to work out a plan in my mind and get results on any project I choose?

Through my Lookabout window, I see a world to explore and know I have the freedom to take charge.

Am I a Lookabout Lion who likes to get results, have lots of choices, and be a free spirit?

*A fellow can't think
or feel accurately
unless he knows
something.*

Mark Twain

Feelabout
Koala
Tugs
Hearts

Feelabout
Koala

When I'm a Feelabout Koala

If I were a Koala, a Feelabout Koala,
you'd find me surrounded by friends.
For I love to chatter
with people who matter.
I hope that the fun never ends.

I help all my friends
to get along well
and help them be part of a team.
With everyone working
and playing together,
I'm flexible, smiling, and serene.

My favorite of places
to sit is the sofa,
surrounded by pillows and rugs.
I'd like to feed everyone
cookies and cocoa,
cheerfully giving them hugs.

I love to do nice things for my friends,
especially give gifts to them.

But tell me you're angry,
or bluster and yell,
and you'll find me shrinking away.
Don't make me feel silly
and shove me around,
or I'll struggle to get my own way.

"Poor me!" can be snappy,
whiny, and prickly
when I am feeling left out.
To get me involved,
praise my help with some friends.
Believe me, you don't have to shout.

I love to sit in a cozy chair and daydream
about happy people helping one another.

Just give me a part
to play in each game,
with everyone getting along.
A crowd where people
are working together
will help me to feel I belong.

I love to have harmony,
smiling and sweet.
I sing when I'm part of the plan.
And I hunger for compliments
coming from you;
they make me feel precious and grand.

I love parties and the gentle laughter of my friends
while we all eat together.

Feelabout Koala

When I'm a Feelabout kind of person,
I need to feel in harmony with
everything around me,
that my feelings matter and I belong.

I like to... *(check the boxes most like you)*

☐ learn by doing and making things with my hands.

☐ hug and be hugged by people I like.

☐ have noisy fun.

☐ know everybody is a friend to me.

☐ dance all around to music.

☐ ride my bike fast, feeling the wind on my face and the movement of my body.

☐ wear clothes that are neat, but it's okay for me to get them dirty or rumpled.

☐ listen only as long as I want to.

☐ sit in any chair I want, whenever I want.

☐ feel it's okay to let everyone know how I feel.

☐ work on something right away and think about what I'm doing as I go along.

☐ not have to pay attention to the clock.

Feelabout You

Whom have **I** helped who appreciated what I did?

Who are the people **I** like to be with?

What sorts of things do **I** like to make with my hands?

Am I someone who loves to make things? And when I know that everyone around me is friendly, do I like to share my feelings and talk?

Through my Feelabout window, I feel how to create harmony and help friends get along with one another.

Am I a Feelabout Koala who likes to touch things, feel in balance and be with my friends?

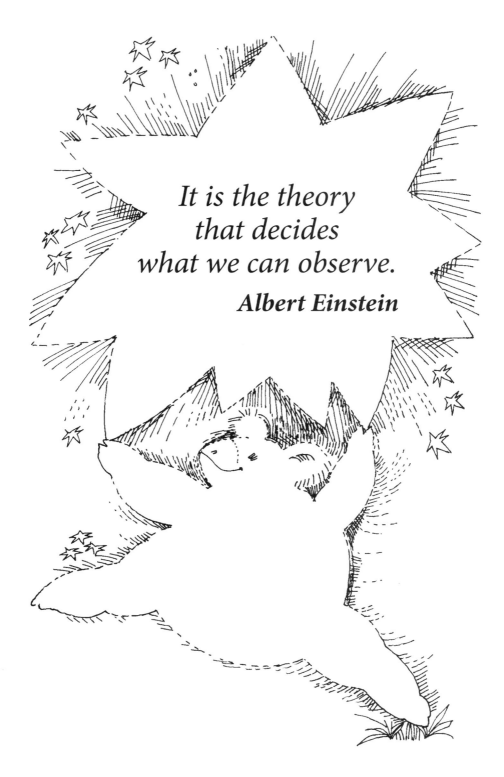

*It is the theory
that decides
what we can observe.*

Albert Einstein

The Synergy Pal Most Like You

Now you know whether you are a Thinkabout, Lookabout, Talkabout, or Feelabout kind of person most of the time. Each person has his or her own natural talents, which is a certain way of belonging in the world.

But you are, also, probably a little like the other three Synergy Pals. You are really at your best when you bring *all* the parts together, from the inside out. That's how you create synergy, working with all of your parts—your Synergy Pals.

Your Natural Talents

And now for an easy quiz to learn about your natural "thinking" talents. It's not a test, though; it's a series of questions to find your natural talents in thinking. All you have to know is you—the way you most like to be, your urges, the actions you like to take in the world, what you're willing to do, and what is important to you that is, your personality.

Your personality has an overall pattern that tells you what you're willing to do and how you make sense of what others do. Understanding, order, freedom, and harmony, are the four different core values we'll be working with. As with the Synergy Pals, one is likely your main personality, but all play a part in who you are.

Take some time to think about the following questions and answer them carefully. They'll tell you what you want to know. Every answer is right.

Thinkabout   Lookabout   Talkabout   Feelabout

Answer the questions according to the very strongest feelings you have about each one. This is the easiest and most natural way for you to understand the creative circle of your own values—understanding, order, freedom, and harmony. Thinking is fun when we are aware of our values and feelings.

How you like to act when you think, see, hear, and feel is important. We are born to choose what is most true for us, so our quiz answers are always correct, as long as we are honest.

Because other people have different talents and think, see, hear, and feel things differently, they will answer the questions differently.

After you have finished the quiz, you may find it interesting and fun to talk about your different answers with your friends.

**For each question,
consider how you feel.**

Give a four (4) to the answer **MOST** like you.

Give a three (3) to the answer **next-to-most** like you.

Give a two (2) to the answer **next-to-least** like you.

Give a one (1) to the answer **LEAST** like you.

Don't use the same number twice.

Here's an example of how to answer the questions:

I like...

a. to have things
in Order my way.

> **2**
> The answer next-to-least like me.

b. the Freedom to
get things done.

> **1**
> The answer least like me.

c. the Harmony of
getting along with
my best friends.

> **4**
> The answer most like me.

d. Understanding my
inspired dreams
in a new way.

> **3**
> The answer next-most like me.

1. I feel happiest with myself when I am…

a. helping my friends get along together
and being thanked for my help .... ☐

b. putting my belongings in order so
I can find things when I need them .. ☐

c. sharing my new ideas to inspire
others to seek their own new ideas............. ☐

d. visualizing a plan and explaining
how to get it done quickly and correctly .... ☐

2. I work best when I can…

a. work with others and be shown
how to do things by someone
who knows how.. ☐

b. think and work quietly on my own,
following directions step by step .... ☐

c. watch what someone else does well,
plan how I will do it, and get it done........... ☐

d. tell others my new ideas, inspiring them
to risk doing things in a new way .... ☐

**Add up the numbers going down in each
column of boxes. Put the total in the
matching box at the bottom of the page.**

☐ ☐ ☐ ☐

3. When I'm with others talking and listening, I...

a. first watch and listen, then freely share my big plan about when, what, why and how to do it ....

b. first enthusiastically tell of my great new ideas, then I want to hear if others understood me ....

c. warmly ask about others' feelings and share my feelings in a friendly, helpful way............................

d. just politely listen until I'm asked what I think; then I quietly answer ...

4. I like stories . . .

a. about real-life problems and solutions that go deeper than usual and that end happily ever after
(Heidi/Scrooge-Christmas Carol) ....

b. about true adventure, mysteries, facts, tried-and-true heroes and heroines
(Harry Potter Series/Charlotte's Web)...

c. about history's great visionaries, inventors who look ahead to create a better future
(Helen Keller/Abe Lincoln Biography)............

d. that explore magical things, faraway places, and people with different beliefs
(Alice in Wonderland/The Wizard of Oz) ....

Add up the numbers going down in each column of boxes. Put the total in the matching box at the bottom of the page.

5. I solve my problems or make decisions best when….

a. I feel secure enough working in a group to ask other people to help me..........................

b. I know the facts that tell me exactly what to do to get the right answer....

c. I plan things my own way by comparing good and bad ideas to get quick results.. ......

d. I brainstorm with others, trust hunches, and discover a new way to put ideas together...............................

6. I like to play games that…

a. allow everyone loads of action, where no one loses (*heart2heart/playground/skateboard*)........................

b. have rules and lots of action to watch, where someone wins (*Monopoly™/football*)...........................

c. allow me to direct, think, or plan ahead (*Chess/Follow-the-Leader*) ....

d. let me act things out or use my imagination (*Pictionary™/charades*)...............

Add up the numbers going down in each column of boxes. Put the total in the matching box at the bottom of the page.

7. I learn best when…

a. I can bend the rules in a new way, discovering things for myself .... ☐

b. I can practice skills I already know while carefully following instructions... ☐

c. someone helps me by showing me the easiest way to get things done .... ☐

d. I can think ideas through, plan, set goals, and get the job done in my own time .... ☐

8. Sometimes, I don't want to…

a. hurt your feelings, because it disrupts **HARMONY**. I avoid conflict at all costs, by not telling the truth, blaming, hiding my feelings and burying old hurts deep inside myself .... ☐

b. finish the things I start, because the details are boring. When I'm excited about something new, I feel inspired, **UNDERSTANDING** a great new idea .... ☐

c. be gentle and considerate of others' feelings, because I'll lose my **FREEDOM** to get results .... ☐

d. feel rushed to make decisions when I don't know all the facts, fearing I'll lose the **ORDER** I need to feel safe ... ☐

Add up the numbers going down in each column of boxes. Put the total in the matching box at the bottom of the page. ☐ ☐ ☐ ☐

Now, let's add up the results.

First, add together the totals in each column on each of the four pages. Enter the numbers in the boxes below.

Column totals from **1st page**: ☐ ☐ ☐ ☐

Column totals from **2nd page**: ☐ ☐ ☐ ☐

Column totals from **3rd page**: ☐ ☐ ☐ ☐

Column totals from **4th page**: ☐ ☐ ☐ ☐

ADD **COLUMN TOTALS** ☐ ☐ ☐ ☐

Owl   Lion   Chimp   Koala

Next, you must **divide each COLUMN TOTAL by 2**.

For example, if the total in the OWL box is 22,
divide 22 by 2 which gives you a new total of 11 (22÷2 = 11).
If the total in the OWL box is 23, the new total would be 11½.
(Halves are okay!)

Thinkabout **OWL** total divided by 2	**Lookabout** **LION** total divided by 2	**Talkabout** **CHIMP** total divided by 2	**Feelabout** **KOALA** total divided by 2
☐	☐	☐	☐

On the page after next you'll find the four animals around a tree's growth rings.

On that page, **color** in the same number of growth rings as your final total for each animal.

For example:
If you have 11 as your final Thinkabout Owl total,
color 11 growth rings out from the center of the tree trunk in
the Thinkabout Owl section.

 Color the rings of the **Thinkabout Owl** section **grassy green**. The orderly, analytical part of you is like grass — growing steadily and quietly.

 Color the rings of the **Lookabout Lion** section **sky blue**. The free-spirited visual part of you is like the cool, blue, wide open sky.

 Color the rings of the **Talkabout Chimp** section **sunny yellow**. The understanding, auditory part of you is like the bright light of the energizing sun.

 Color the rings of the **Feelabout Koala** section **earthy red**. The harmonious kinesthetic part of you is like the warm, comforting, friendly earth.

This is the center, or core, of your wholehearted feelings and deeply-rooted values of well-being—the rings of life.

heart2heart
Be Yourself — Everyone Else Is Taken

Thinkabout Owl
(Green)

Lookabout Lion
(Blue)

If you have more green rings, you like facts and like to put things in order. You work towards perfection and want the world to be a safe place. You have trouble expressing your fears, feelings, and opinions without criticizing yourself and others.

If you have more blue rings, you like to look at your surroundings to see how things could be better. You like to act on a plan rather than a feeling. You lead others to get results. You don't accept others' limits of themselves.

If you have more red rings, you follow feelings about things and use intuition. You are quiet, friendly, and helpful. You like peaceful moments, to feel you belong, and to make things. You have trouble expressing fear and anger. You hold worry inside, and lack of focus means stress to you.

If you have more yellow rings, you like to talk about ideas and get reactions. You like to interact and hear how ideas sound. You express excitement, anger and love and want understanding. You like everyone to have fun talking. You feel stress when your motives are misunderstood.

Feelabout Koala
(Red)

Talkabout Chimp
(Yellow)

Deeply-rooted core values and feelings affect thinking, revealing your natural talents. The section with the most colored rings is your special *inside* self, your *inside color*.

Synergy Pals Profile

a logical grass green

think about owl

feel about koala

an earthy feeling red

Color from the inside out,

Your Core Talents

lookabout lion

1 2 3 4 5 6 7 8 9 10 11 12 13 14 15 16

a visionary blue

talkabout chimp

a sunny idea yellow

just the way a tree grows from its heart.

Feelabout Koala and Talkabout Chimp would rather feel than think. Thinkabout Owl and Lookabout Lion prefer logical thinking. Thinkabout Owl and Feelabout Koala like a slower pace, waiting for things to happen before they decide or until an idea catches in their minds. They learn by doing things hands-on. Lookabout Lions do things they can get done, and Talkabout Chimps make up their minds quickly, taking risks to create solutions; they tend to see the big picture.

Look again at the growth rings you colored. Is one section larger and stronger than the others? Or are they all about the same?

If you are like most people, you have two sections that are stronger. It's important to have strong natural talents that you can rely on.

Having really strong natural talents also means you have other talents that you rarely use and may have trouble understanding, especially in other people. But the whole of you is your strong talents plus your less-used ones. And the whole of the world is people with the same strong talents plus people with other talents (like your less-used ones).

We need to *think*, *see*, *hear*, and *feel* all of our natural talents, both *inside* and *outside*, so our growth is balanced and our own tree of life grows straight and tall.

The chart on the next page compares our root values and natural talents. It's natural for us to favor one or two talents over others. Notice how the Thinkabout Owl and Lookabout Lion prefer *thinking* over *feeling* while Feelabout Koala and Talkabout Chimp prefer *feeling* over *thinking*.

Thinkabout Owl and Feelabout Koala are like each other because they prefer to take on things more slowly, in an introverted, inside-sort-of-way.

Lookabout Lion and Talkabout Chimp are just the opposite. They prefer faster answers and doing things in an extroverted, outside-sort-of-way.

On the next page, **outline** the quarter section of the tree that corresponds to your strongest talent in the approprite color. If your strongest section is blue, outline the Lookabout square in blue. Then color **inside** this large section with the color of our second strongest talent. For example, if your largest ring is blue and second largest ring is yellow, outline the Lookabout section in blue and fill it in with yellow.

Team up with your less-preferred talents

Thinkabout Owl
(Green)

Lookabout Lion
(Blue)

look about lion

THINK

WATCH

thinkabout owl

FinishWork : **Knowledge**
Calm Colors : **Cool Colors**
Neat : **Messy**
Order : **Freedom**
Facts, Safety : Choices, Results

Think things over, take : Implement plans, make
time, answer questions, : decisions, answer questions,
listen, and watch : and instruct others.

Action : **Inspired**
Warm Colors : **Bright Colors**
Neat : **Messy**
Harmony : **Understanding**
Belonging, Activity : Ideas, Creativity

Feel things, take time, ask : Take risks, make
questions, : decisions, answer
and ask : questions, and
others : create new
: ideas.

TELL

talkabout chimp

FEEL

feelabout koala

Feelabout Koala
(Red)

Talkabout Chimp
(Yellow)

How does each part of you do what it does best?

We all have lots of different ways of being smart, all using our inner and outer talents.

Thinkabout Owl (Green)
Earth Keeper finds the right growth way

Lookabout Lion (Blue)
Star Leader shapes the future way

Feelabout Koala (Red)
Peace Maker loves the easy active way

Talkabout Chimp (Yellow)
Dream Mover seeks a new imaginative way

When these close pals team up and work together in different ways, they show us how to use our unique internal strengths in the world. We can achieve much more by working together with everyone's sharp strengths, especially when they are different from ours. That's how we get synergy. New ideas may emerge and we can change the world.

Rings of Life

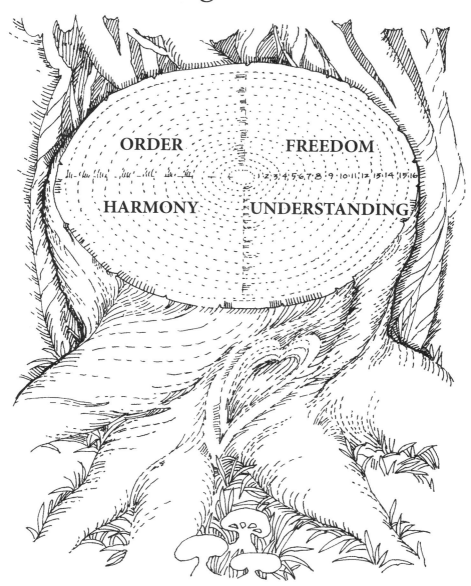

ORDER   FREEDOM

1 2 3 4 5 6 7 8 9 10 11 12 13 14 15 16

HARMONY   UNDERSTANDING

We all need strong roots and good support to stretch and grow, adding new skills on top of previous ones. Our strong roots come from our lasting values—what matters to us most.

We learn to stretch and grow on the *inside* and work and belong together on the *outside*. Our stretching uncovers our own true roots and helps us understand the rings of life.

On the next page, outline the large square with your animal's color — green, blue, yellow, or red.

☼♡ If your strongest growth ring is blue, outline the large Lookabout square. Then *inside* this large blue square, outline the small square with the color of your second-largest growth ring.

☼♡ If your second strongest ring is yellow, then outline the small Talkabout square yellow *inside* the large Lookabout blue square.

☼♡ Look at the smaller square you outlined, which shows your second-largest growth ring. Do the characteristics seem familiar and important to you? These are your deeply-rooted values — your emotional core.

We can learn a lot from understanding our deeply-rooted values, as well as others' values. We can understand how thought, experience, and feeling fit together. Interacting, we discover happiness comes from the inside out.

When all four senses work together well, something called synergy occurs. Interdependence (working together) is always more productive than independence (working alone).

When people ask you what you want to be when you grow up, you might talk to a grownup about this chart.

Thinkabout Owl   Lookabout Lion

Think • Envision • Self-Contained • Left Brain

Researcher Strategic Planner Technician Manager	Systems Analyst Designer Manufacturer Program Developer
Adventurer Mechanic Artisan Quality Controller	Entrepreneur Theorist Pioneer Sales Person

Ask • Listen • Watch • Reflect • Input • Slower to get things done

Tell • Show • Express • Output • Get things done quickly

Feel • Create • Relate • Right Brain

Feelabout Koala   Talkabout Chimp

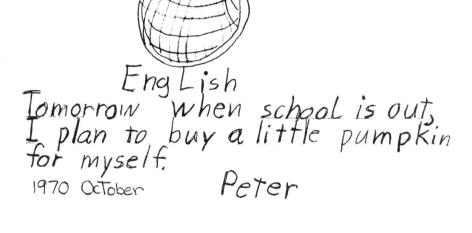

English
Tomorrow when school is out,
I plan to buy a little pumpkin
for myself.
1970 October   Peter

Peter, strategically planning
when he was eight.
Now he plans virtual tunnels very well.

Alex loves bonding
and family reunions

"A poem in a child
there always is to be.
A poem in a child
is always to go free."

— *Liza Reverman Dansky (eight years old)*
*Liza contemplates loving relationships
and feels joyful, full and free!*

"In my dream, the angel shrugged and said,
"If we fail this time, it will be a failure of
imagination" and then she placed the world
gently in the palm of my hand."

— *Brian Andreas, Imagining World*

Draw upon the brains of successful people…

We ride on the shoulders of the Great Thinkers who have come before us, giving us strong roots and good support to stretch and grow, adding new skills to previous ideas. We all need meaning and purpose, so we study things that interest our common senses. Look up some of the discoveries made by our great world thinkers! Discover your strengths.

Smarter Together

Turn Conflict into Cooperation

Do unto others as they'd like done unto them

When we introduced the Synergy Pals to you, we told you about each one—what they do, how they behave, what they need. Then we helped you identify which Synergy Pal you are.

But Sometimes how you behave and what you need create problems when you are with other people. You're just being you, but that doesn't seem to work all of the time.

In this section, we identify the problems that might happen when you are with other people, people who are a different Synergy Pal from you or even the same one. And we tell you some of the ways to make being with others better.

Working together can work—with just a little understanding.

Whole Mind, Happy Heart

Thinkabout Owl
(Green)

Lookabout Lion
(Blue)

ORDER

look about lion

FREEDOM

thinkabout owl

*I need time
to figure it out.*

My Lesson:

RISK starting
without a plan or
all the facts.

SHARE my feelings.

STRETCH my
boundaries.

I am contemplative at my best,
critical at my worst.

*I need to
act on plans.*

My Lesson:

RISK working
more slowly.

SHARE and listen to
my feelings and words.

STRETCH to accept what
others offer.

I am decisive at my best,
defiant at my worst.

*I need to be
part of the group.*

My Lesson:

RISK being honest
about my needs.

SHARE my dreams.

STRETCH to take charge.

I provide good
service at my
best, am lazy
at my worst.

*I need to question and
communicate.*

My Lesson:

RISK getting organized.

SHARE the work.

STRETCH to plan ahead.

I am enthusiastic
at my best,
unfocused at
my worst.

talkabout chimp

HARMONY

feelabout koala

UNDERSTANDING

Feelabout Koala
(Red)

Talkabout Chimp
(Yellow)

Talkabout Chimp Understands

Feelings
are satisfied with

Understanding
Ideas
Creativity

"Let me tell you about this fantastic
new idea. Tell me what you think of it."

Talkabout Chimp's Pals say:

Let's play with it and see what happens if we do it differently.

Given what we know is true, maybe…

Let's find out what's on the other side of that mountain.

Talkabout Chimp is matter-of-fact…

…with the Thinkabout Owl pal

What Works? What Hurts? What's the Solution?

Plan ahead to relieve our fears.
To avoid fools' blame games.
Walk and talk our worries clear,
When our ideas are not the same.

Your lists are "honey-do".
Each to ourselves for that.
Sometimes I bend the rules,
To evade details you map.

If you reject me it hurts.
I retreat, unsure,
Ignoring's the worst
I ever have to endure.

Yet we share the need for a happy home.
You meet everyday tasks head on, while I freely roam.

Talkabout Chimp takes risks…

…with
the Lookabout
Lion pal

What Works? What Hurts? What's the Solution?

I don't get your attention.
All things exist to teach
My feelings go so very deep.
What I know is out of reach.

Beyond dreams I know
Inspires magic to say,
I want to talk with you.
Yet I cannot find a way.

Everything to you is logical
Ideas to me surreal.
In everything I imagine
Visions may seem real.

The inspiration I feel makes new projects great.
Our ideas really click, together we create.

Talkabout Chimp uses playfulness…

…with the Feelabout Koala pal

What Works? What Hurts? What's the Solution?

We play in fun-filled ways,
Inside and outside the box.
Change breaks our safe gaze.
Less is more — in this you rock.

Hope is dashed
As our hearts weep,
Of broken promises
One didn't keep.

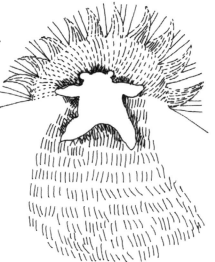

I know just how you feel,
I need you to know about me.
I'd like to spend our time
In peaceful harmony.

Your welcome words make me feel
good, when I visit your friendly neighborhood.

Talkabout Chimp
jump-starts new understanding…

…with the
Talkabout
Chimp
pal

What Works? What Hurts? What's the Solution?

When our words come together,
We find we're much the same.
To exchange bright ideas
Is our meaning-making game.

Please listen to me politely,
Sometimes I feel neglected.
Won't you please hear me?
So the message is not rejected.

Creating well with others,
How nice to be with you.
We walk and talk together,
We're sensitive and true.

The truth is plain in time and space.
Believe in love's happy ending in a rainbow place.

For grownups who work and play with the Synthesis Learner...

Chimp's values are Understanding and Fun

- Learns by reorganizing
- Has many good answers
- Relies on creativity
  - Is it original?
  - Does it make sense?
  - Is it expressive?

Tips for Caregivers

How best to help Talkabout Chimps

- Promote their ideas
- Be a resource
- Become an evaluator
- Serve as facilitator
- Encourage innovation
- Let them explain
- Be the storyteller

Talkabout Chimp
as Student

I love to share my far-out thoughts,
to speak out and have fun.
You'll find me in the spotlight
before the day is done.
It's hard for me to fit myself into
a routine pace.
So please respect my feelings.
I need unstructured space.

Talkabout Chimp
as Teacher

I love to be creative, to watch my students grow.
I bring excitement to the class. The magic starts to show.
My approach is quite unstructured, unpredictable, as well.
Make believe or democracy — to teach these things is swell.

Talkabout Chimp says:

I'm quick to anger,
  fast to talk,
    because the words
    are real.
      I sense injustice,
      moral outrage,
        about the pain I feel.
      To find the need,
      to fix the pain,
      I'll take the risk
      to make our world
      more sane.

For when the upset's over an outrageous story remains. We get lots of courageous ideas from brave lessons. Serious or hilarious, a story is a journey of feelings to discover we may be delirious.

Talkabout Chimp
is an idea-starter

When I'm threatened,
I may act...

Scattered
Let-down
Overwhelmed
Pushy
Naïve
Worried

I need to learn
how to...

Organize details
Follow through, focus
Plan ahead
Listen to others
Be practical
Give jobs to others

...because I feel bad.   **...to feel good.**

Talkabout Chimp
needs to question and communicate.

I FEEL	Misunderstood.
WHEN	Others don't listen to my inspired ideas or share my playful mood.
BECAUSE	I value understanding and I need to direct myself and seek new rules.
I MUST RISK	Losing inspiration to be organized.
AND SHARE	The work that can be delegated.
AND STRETCH	To plan ahead and finish step by step.

If your heart could talk about UNDERSTANDING

Save Talkabout Chimp from a

Heartache

by UNDERSTANDING how to
create ideas in a new and fun way

Heartlight

A little change of heart can be
the biggest change of all.

One Thing in Common

Match and Mismatch
Ways to interact with
Talkabout Chimp

 Lookabout **with** Talkabout

Match in both being VISION QUESTERS for the big picture thinkers

But Lookabout Lion maybe is too IMPATIENT

 Feelabout **with** Talkabout

Match in both
LISTENING TO OTHER IDEAS—why people do things

But Feelabout Koala May LACK FOLLOW-THROUGH

 Thinkabout **with** Talkabout

Match in both
SEARCHING FOR ANSWERS within values

But Thinkabout Owl maybe is too PESSIMISTIC to get started

Talkabout **with** Talkabout

Match in both being
CREATIVE DREAMERS to ignite ideas

But both Talkabout Chimps may have poor FOLLOW-THROUGH

Thinkabout Owl
Loves Order

**Feelings
are satisfied by**

Order
Facts
Safety

"Once we get all the facts in order,
we'll know the best way to do things."

Thinkabout Owl's pals say:

Here's what we already know. I can see how the information fits into this project.

Even if it isn't broken, can't we still make it better?

$\pi = 3.14$

I've been thinking. We know enough about it to try something new.

Thinkabout Owl is a cool onlooker. . .

What Works? What Hurts? What's the Solution?

...with the Feelabout Koala pal

Methodical systems are my tools,
Tradition, goals, my true-blue friends.
You use too few exacting rules.
Your flip flop moods
like rubber bend.

You free up fun,
it brings us ease,
Win or lose in
competition games.
Clear rules — a little
quieter, please.
Loud action your way, mine
is tame.

Clutter up my
need for tidiness,
Please think problems
to the end.
I'm embarrassed
by the mess.
Then off you go
leaving me to fend.

However, in your
random acts of kindness,
flexible as a noodle,
you always bend.

Thinkabout Owl
gets to the point at a steady pace…

…with the
Lookabout
Lion pal

What Works? What Hurts? What's the Solution?

You're way up in the future. Come down to earth right now,
To show off your witty humor. I need you here and HOW.

About how to use my time.
I know you plan big dreams for me.
Seek wild grand demands.
Please just let me free to be.

To fulfill my steady dreams,
If I'm allowed to shine,
Learn useful skills, not weird
extremes.

Write details to list your steps in line seems wise, to
make our numbers add up fine.

Thinkabout Owl
finds order when we need it…

…with the
Thinkabout
Owl pal

What Works? What Hurts? What's the Solution?

Our relationship is brilliant.
We support each other well.
We both enjoy the rules of home
All the order is just swell.

The tradition of our family tree
brightens up our careful life.
Stability, we do agree,
brings comfort without strife.

We get along so very well,
Daily rules we always see.
Tasks require work each day.
Happily in skills we do agree.

Educated action reminds us to
avoid analysis paralysis,
as our deliberate life unwinds.

Thinkabout Owl challenges risky ideas…

What Works? What Hurts? What's the Solution?

…with the
Talkabout
Chimp pal

We both help our minds to shift
From humdrum to optimistic.
Our good fit of differing gifts
Makes bold dreams realistic.

I count on dependable tools,
I have a zeal to plan every day.
If you push more sensible rules,
Storyboard tells of our idea play.

Practical senses busy my days,
Eco cycles urge much mirth.
Reveals the sun's
golden rays,
As raindrops
race down to earth.

Imaginations stir your mind.
We do everything in a new way, until I can barely unwind.

For grownups who work and play with the Fact Finder...

Thinkabout Owl

Owl's values are Order and Safety

- ♡ Learns by remembering
- ♡ Answers are always clear
- ♡ Relies on organizing
  (facts, definitions, steps in a procedure)

Tips for Caregivers

How best to help Thinkabout Owls

- Show them how they are right
- Give direct instruction
- Use knowledge to increase comprehension
- Break work into steps

"Whoo, what, where, when, how, why?"

Thinkabout Owl as Student

I love my school, respect its rules. I need routine and order. I'm punctual, dependable. You know I am a learner. I share in all the duties that I'm told we all should do. I want our subjects plainly taught. I need to hear from you.

Thinkabout Owl as Teacher

My teaching style is clearly geared to order and routine. I am consistent in my way. My students are a team. I teach them what our country stands for, the duties we all share. I discipline when necessary. I know I'm firm and fair.

Thinkabout Owl says:

Though I'm very slow to anger,
I really have no buffer.
I criticize and blame myself,
then spin my wheels and suffer.
I feel stuck when I am cornered,
until I pull my self together
and move forward with brave pluck.

Thinkabout Owl
is a caretaker

When threatened,
I may act…

Aloof
Picky
Stuck
Bored
Stubborn
Suspicious

I need to learn
how to…

Express my feelings
Be spontaneous
Just get started
Enjoy unstructured time
Get along with active people
Trust others' decisions

… because I feel bad.   **…to feel good.**

Thinkabout Owl
needs time to figure it out.

I FEEL	Cornered and stubborn.
WHEN	Others push or criticize me.
BECAUSE	I value order and conformity. I need a quiet, safe place to work and play.
I MUST RISK	Starting without rules in order to be creative.
AND SHARE	My feelings and be kind.
AND STRETCH	My boundaries for having fun.

If your heart could talk
about ORDER

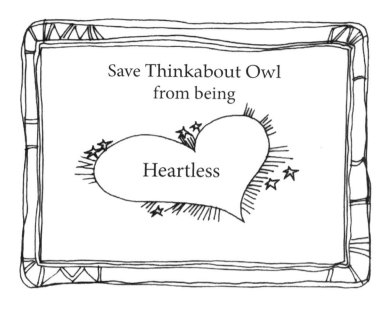

Save Thinkabout Owl
from being

Heartless

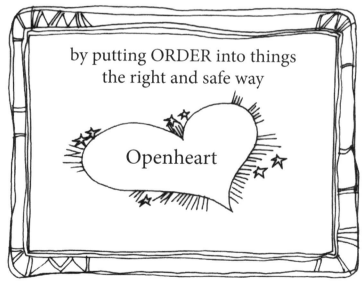

by putting ORDER into things
the right and safe way

Openheart

A little change of heart can be
the biggest change of all.

One Thing in Common

Match and Mismatch
Way to Interact with
Thinkabout Owl

Lookabout **with** Thinkabout

Match in because both
GET THINGS DONE—
focus on order and structure

But Lookabout Lion maybe is beyond analysis to synthesis

Feelabout **with** Thinkabout

Match because both need
HARMONY

But Feelabout Koala may lack FOCUS

Talkabout **with** Thinkabout

Match because both like
BEING DIRECT and on target

But Talkabout Chimp relishes CHANGE

Thinkabout **with** Thinkabout

Match in because both
PRACTICE CAREFULLY and
FOCUS ON STRUCTURE

But Thinkabout Owls may both want to BE RIGHT

Lookabout Lion
Needs Freedom

**Feelings are
satisfied by**

Freedom
Choices
Results

"We'll get somewhere only if we choose what we
want to have happen."

Lookabout Lion's pals say:

I've carefully looked at the problem overall. Here's what we can do.

Let's make a model to see if the parts will work.

I understand what we're trying to do. There may be more than one way to do it.

Lookabout Lion plans things...

... with the Talkabout Chimp pal

What Works? What Hurts? What's the Solution?

Clear rules reduce chaos
Hardships urge creativity.
In times we seek change
Challenges adapt our flexibility.

You encircle family ties,
I take off by myself.
My mind quests for
knowledge
From books upon
the shelf.

At times we walk and talk.
We grant freedom to explore.
Minds seek an educated guess.
Big thoughts we both adore.

To be my own true self, differs from your own.
I'm distant — at times alone.

Lookabout Lion finds new plans...

...with the
Thinkabout
Owl pal

What Works? What Hurts? What's the Solution?

Opposites attract, may attack.
But the thing I love we do:
Embody opposites for variety.
Family is dear to you.

Between anxiety and boredom
We respect opposing motion.
Where creativity flourishes,
Yet you show no emotion.

Follow to a place we match.
That is safety and security.
To make our future plans hatch:
Do the work or let me be.

I travel among the wonders
to bring a new idea to view.

Lookabout Lion designs models...

...with the
Feelabout
Koala
pal

What Works? What Hurts? What's the Solution?

You are very physical,
Action for you is swell.
Fun for me is mental,
On ideas I like to dwell.

I am future-focused,
On this we do agree.
We love each other
dearly,
As everyone can see.

You live in the now,
Funny and very clever.
Cast us heart to heart,
The coolest pals ever.

My mind lives out in space,
yet you pull me back to earth's tether.

Lookabout Lion is a freedom fighter…

What Works? What Hurts? What's the Solution?

We love to be inventive.
Our wisdom left to shine,
Our vision-logic grows.
We are, after all, of one mind.

Yet distant with each other,
Because we're
independent.
We cheer each other on,
To be quite resplendent.

I want to be as strong
as you,
You're the one in charge.
It seems we do compete
In matters small and large.

In tug of war, gender gaps can cause a rift,
if we clash in cycles of our life.

For grownups who work and play with the Confident Learner...

Lookabout Lion

Lion's values are Freedom and Results

- ☼ Learns by reasoning
- ☼ May have several good answers
- ☼ Relies on reason:

    Is something clearly stated?
    Is something true?
    Is something relevant?
    Is it complete?

Tips for Caregivers

How to best help Lookabout Lions

- Give them slack
- Become a coach
- Build models
- Involve them
- Give immediate feedback
- Provide the freedom to act

Prove it.

$\pi = 3.14$

Lookabout Lion as Student

I love to look inside a thought
to see just how it works.
I love to work all by myself
to find out all the quirks.
I'm logical, I'm curious,
I need to understand.
It makes me happy
when you tell me just
how good I am.

Lookabout Lion as Teacher

I seek to answer nature's riddles, and help you do the same. To give you useful information is my highest aim. I inspire you to stretch your mind, to find an answer rare. I create new ways of teaching you. I really, truly care.

Lookabout Lion Says:

I'm quick to anger — step aside!
My fury is volcanic.
I tend to zap the calmer one,
and this can make you panic,
but then it's over and forgotten.
I'm on to other things.
If you can move along with me,
then we can do great things.

Lookabout Lion
is a born leader

When I'm threatened I may act…

Bossy
Blunt
Unfeeling
Serious
Demanding
Like I "know it all"

… because I feel bad.

I need to learn how to…

Be less demanding
Consider others' needs
Listen to feelings
Be more fun and creative
Relax and slow down
Poke fun at myself
Laugh with others

… to feel good.

Lookabout Lion
needs to act on plans, to direct others.

I FEEL	Blocked.
WHEN	Others avoid decision and follow-through to finish tasks.
BECAUSE	I value freedom to act and I need to do new things and get results.
I MUST RISK	Working more slowly to be fun-loving and considerate.
AND SHARE	And listen to others' feelings and words.
AND STRETCH	To accept what others offer, and enjoy each other more.

Heart 2 Heart

If your heart could talk about FREEDOM

Save Lookabout Lion
from being

Hardhearted

by giving FREEDOM
to do things their own way

Braveheart

A little change of heart can be
the biggest change of all.

One Thing in Common

Match and Mismatch
Ways to interact with Lookabout Lion

Feelabout **with** Lookabout

Match in both being
ADVENTUROUS—control own actions to
meet goals

But Feelabout Koala may need PRACTICAL ACTION

Thinkabout **with** Lookabout

Match in both wanting
TASKS DONE WELL—structured, order and
organization

But Thinkabout Owl may be SLOW TO ACT—analysis
paralysis

Talkabout **with** Lookabout

Match in both being
CLEVER in symbolic awareness

But Talkabout Chimp may feel MISUNDERSTOOD

Lookabout **with** Lookabout

Match in both being
SELF-CONFIDENT AND CAPABLE

But both Lookabout Lions may be INSENSITIVE and take
charge to control actions

Feelabout Koala
Wants Harmony

**Feelings
are satisfied by**

Harmony
Belonging
Hands-On

"I made it just for you. I knew you'd like it."

Feelabout Koala's pals say:

You have to handle things with just the force required. Not more or less.

We can build it together if we all lend a hand.

It's okay the way it is, but let's move a few things around a little. It won't hurt it.

Feelabout Koala is fun in action…

…with the Thinkabout Owl pal

What Works?
What Hurts?
What's the Solution?

I like risks in spontaneity.
About fun we disagree.
Yet we agree predictably
Some order sets us free.

For you it's right or wrong,
Whereas I don't care at all.
I like to have a lot of fun,
Together we'll have a ball.

Win-win can be
tactical,
Our roles are not
the same.
Together we are practical,
Let's play no hassle games.

We share hope for happy families,
yet clear goals respect our flexibilities.

Feelabout Koala finds the easy ways...

...with the
Lookabout Lion
pal

What Works? What Hurts? What's the Solution?

We are very competent,
Your focus laser steady.
Practical goals I protect.
Logic when we're ready.

I live joy here and now,
In action is good enough.
Risk is not picture perfect
In traction pain is tough.

In future goals and dreams
Your mind seems far away.
I do not need the future
To be better than today.

My "hands-on" and your "heads-up" are swell.
Friends get clever tasks done together rather well.

Feelabout Koala boosts others...

...with the Talkabout Chimp pal

What Works? What Hurts? What's the Solution?

Brain teasers teach us,
Sages give new shows.
I'm very independent,
As you already know.

To become better
New ideas risk ire.
If secret is teachable
Moods stay unriled.

You get " it," whatever "it" is.
Fans clap hands, that's cool.
Race ahead in word and deed,
Think big earns fame's tool.

Questions run deep; how nice to be with you.
Help and play with others, we're sensitive and true.

Feelabout Koala finds harmony…

…with the
Feelabout Koala
pal

What Works? What Hurts? What's the Solution?

"Eco" friendly time together
Change feeds our mind to grow.
Mother nature loves everything.
Chaos exists in survival's flow.

To be just who you are,
Drives our talents' needs.
We find it's scary to be at odds.
Hearts warm when friends meet.

We love to change together,
Turning points bring us luck.
We understand each other,
Ready, fire, aim, then duck.

Our energies flow, super-charged with need,
because success builds bridges to explore new deeds.

For grownups who work and play with the
Teamwork Learner…

Feelabout
Koala

Koala's values are Harmony and Cooperation

♡ Learns by relating
♡ Wants answers that are easily understood
♡ Relies on harmony:
Does it show connection with others?
Does it charm others?
Does it value cooperation?

Tips for Caregivers

How to best help Feelabout Koalas

• Show how they are liked
• Focus their high energy, enthusiasm
• Use the discussion approach
• Bond through activities
• Be a motivator
• Build follow-through
• Organize
• Prioritize

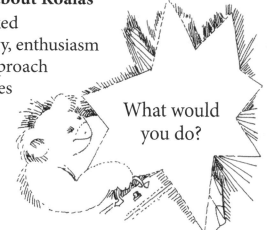

What would
you do?

Feelabout Koala
as Student

I am impulsive and physical. I want a lot of action.
I make good use of what I learn. I like the competition. I learn by doing with my hands. I love to work with tools. When conflicts come, though, I withdraw.
Fighting is for fools.

Feelabout Koala
as Teacher

The information that I teach is useful here and now. I do not plan, but what I do excites each one— and how! My teaching style's dynamic. I act quickly when I must. I have rapport, and lots of joy. I'm harmony that you can trust.

Feelabout Koala says:

I find it rather difficult to let hurt feelings show.
I'm very easy-going, so you would never know.
I keep it all pent up inside till I can hold no more.
Then please watch out! I may just shout,
To act on what I've stored.

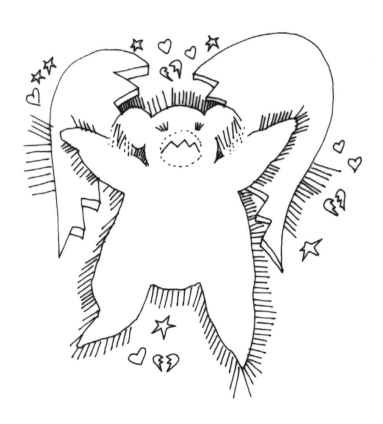

Feelabout Koala
is a shaker and mover

When threatened,
I may act…

I need to learn
how to…

Lonely
Afraid
Gullible
Sneaky
Guilty
Impulsive

Be independent
Be honest about feelings
Be assertive
Be confident
Do good work
Know my boundaries

…because I feel bad.

…to feel good.

Feelabout Koala
needs to be a part of the group

I FEEL	Left out.
WHEN	What I feel and do doesn't seem to matter.
BECAUSE	I value harmony and I need to be a part of what's going on.
I MUST RISK	Being honest about my needs in order to start and finish tasks.
AND SHARE	My decisions, expectations, and boundaries.
AND STRETCH	Myself to lead and risk failure.

Heart 2 Heart

If your heart could talk about HARMONY

Save Feelabout Koala
from having a

Heavyheart

by creating HARMONY
— doing things easily together

Happyheart

A little change of heart can be
the biggest change of all.

One Thing in Common

Match and Mismatch
ways to interact with Feelabout Koala

Lookabout **with** Feelabout

Match because they are
SELF-CONFIDENT

But Lookabout Lions may be too SELF-DISCIPLINED

Thinkabout **with** Feelabout

Match because they are
DEVOTED—task focused

But Thinkabout Owl may be too ORGANIZED

Talkabout **with** Feelabout

Match because they are
COOPERATIVE—good for the group

But Talkabout Chimp may be too INDIRECT with abstract words

Feelabout **with** Feelabout

Match because they are
DRAMATIC—act on what needs to be done

But Feelabout Koala may be too UNFOCUSED

Bringing the Friendly Universe Down to Earth

Talkabout Chimp, Thinkabout Owl, Lookabout Lion, and Feelabout Koala learn lots when they understand each other's feelings. The Synergy Pals show us how to love ourselves, inside and out, and how to love others, too. When we understand each other, we work better together — we create a friendly universe for all.

When we know all of the troubles and face them, we're brave. All of the monsters inside come from fears that we all have, though we often express them in a way that doesn't look like fear. We may feel rejected, neglected, or misunderstood. We might act angry or pretend to know it all.

Our gifts are many, whether we are short or tall, large or small. And in the Friendly Universe, kindness is the finest gift of all.

Synergy
Pals
sum of the
parts

When we work together, using each person's strengths and talents, we create synergy. Synergy gives us greater results from everyone's contributions working together than what we'd get with each one working by himself. So everyone gains. Each feels good by helping out, and all together are producing the best outcome. The sum of the parts creates far stronger results working together.

What is *not* Synergistic?

☼ Too much sameness = no creative action

☼ Too much difference = no agreement

☼ Too much misdirected natural talent = burnout

☼ Unappreciated natural talents = anger, tension, strain

Growing Seasons

Are you a
tiny tree
with a lot of
growing to do?
Or have you
grown a lot
already?

However big or
small we are,
we can always
grow more on
the inside by
learning more
about ourselves
and others.

Although
we can never
completely know
and understand
another person's ideas and experiences, we can all increase
our awareness of the differences.

The following section will help you grow on the inside by
giving you new ways of looking at what goes on in your life.

Seven keys to managing our feelings

1. I can accept that there are unknowns in life.

Choices — I know I can be myself and make up my mind independently, even if I'm different from others.

Disappointments — I can feel okay, even if I don't always understand what's going on around me. I can learn by looking at my mistakes.

Relationships — I can accept other people the way they are, without needing to put them down or give them the cold shoulder to express my hurt. I can appreciate our natural differences.

☼ **In my mind's eye I think that good things will happen.**

I can't always control what will happen to me. These are the unknowns. But I can decide what to do when the unknowns become "knowns," when they happen.

I can also prepare for some. If a test is coming up. I may not know the questions that will be on it, but I can study so I'll know the answers. For other unknowns, I can talk to someone who might help me understand what will happen. If I have to see a doctor, I can ask my mom or dad what the doctor is going to do.

But whether I can prepare for unknowns or not, I can always feel good by being flexible when good or bad things happen to me.

These are the unknowns I can accept in my life:
What would you like to learn more about?

_____

_____

_____

_____

_____

2. **I can stay open to new information and ideas.**

   Choices — I can change my opinion, given new information. I can consider new ideas and treat them as possibilities.

   Disappointments — I can admit my misjudgements, readjust, and allow others to do the same.

   Relationships — I'm willing to listen to what others have to say. I don't need to make others agree with me.

☼ **I can bounce back and learn "aha's" from my mistakes.**

Mistakes are wonderful opportunities for me to learn. They help me figure out how to do better. And they let me know I'm growing on the inside.

Mistakes tell me what not to do next time so I'll know better what *to do*. And others can help me by giving me ideas or suggestions I never thought about.

These are people I can trust to help me when I have a problem.
They do not belittle me but they help me think of solutions.
What have you figured out to do on your own?

_____

_____

_____

_____

3. **I can talk about what hurts, in order to be helpful, instead of repressing my words and thoughts.**

Choices — I can choose my words and tone of voice to say what I mean.

Disappointments — I can expand my range of expression so that others can understand my words better. I can learn from others' misunderstandings.

Relationships — I can listen to and respect what others are trying to say to me. I can understand that there are different expressions and perceptions.

☼ **I reach out to someone who needs comfort.**

When I talk with someone who needs comfort, I am helping that person by saying I care. All problems seem smaller when we share them with another.

When I comfort someone, I am also helping myself. I am learning about how others think and feel. And I feel good inside knowing I am making someone else feel less sad.

When I talk nicely and explain what is bothering me, others can understand me and help me. One time this happened is:

My Friends Support me in unlimited learning. Only I can decide who I am. What we know, what we want to know. What we learned.

_____

_____

_____

_____

4. **I can choose to see the good side of things.**

Choices — I can be creative in life and look for opportunities.

Disappointments — I can accept that bad things happen to good people. I can learn to look for meaning.

Relationships — I can choose to see the good side of others and myself.

☼ **I will look closely at a flower or tree I haven't noticed before.**

Sometimes I am in such a hurry—to get ready for school, to catch the bus, to meet up with friends—that I don't notice what is happening around me. I'm thinking only about what I need to do next or what might happen.

That's a lot of rushing and worrying. If I can slow down, I'll feel calmer. When I stop to look closely at something, such as a flower, I have to slow down and think about what I'm looking at. That looking takes my worries away and helps me see that life has more to it than just what is bothering me.

And sometimes when I slow down I can think better and solve some of my problems.

Even though I may have some problems, I have good things in my life right now. Some of them are:

_____

_____

_____

_____

5. **I can choose to see the funny side of life.**

Choices — I can choose to see life's experiences as an amusing story.

Disappointments — With a sense of humor, I can learn to see the funny side of my setback.

Relationships — I can laugh and learn from my own experiences, and laugh with — not at — others.

☼ **I'm patient with an annoying person, believing we can make things better with laughter.**

When I see someone as annoying, I'm fighting with that person inside me. And sometimes that inside fighting shows on my outside with angry words or worse.

But if I can find something funny to share with that person, then we are together and not fighting any more. And maybe the laughter will push away what I thought was annoying, and I'll see the person as not so bad after all.

I can see in a different way a bad situation in my life or mistake I made. I can even see some humor in it. Here is one situation and what I think is funny enough to laugh about:

If you can't laugh at yourself, you're missing a lot of good laughs.

_____

_____

_____

_____

6. **I can choose to look at details without losing sight of the big picture or plan.**

   Choices — I can seek out information step by step, to solve problems in unusual and creative ways.

   Disappointments — I can learn what happens when I act too quickly on a project that I don't know how to finish.

   Relationships — I can understand the benefits of synergy — working with others who have different talents than I do.

☼ **I can do something special for myself: focus deeply on each detail.**

Working on the details is part of the big picture. I can't finish a project—if I don't pay attention to the little details. I have to complete them if I'm going to be happy with the whole piece when I'm done.

So when I take care of the details, I'm really taking care of me. Doing a careful job from the start with all of the parts means I'll be pleased with the final product. That will make me happy, and that's what I want to be.

First things first. These are the priority details in my life now, the ones I have to take care of before anything else:

Health, education, work, play, relationships, spiritual are a kind of balance wheel always turning to ???? your attention. Put toys away, set the table, help fold clothes.

_____

_____

_____

_____

7. **I can accept what I believe is important while looking at my surroundings with an open mind.**

Choices — I can do what I think is right, not just what others want me to do. I can look at other ways of doing things and choose to be courageous.

Disappointments — I can take pleasure in learning something important, instead of letting fear drive me away.

Relationships — I can set my own boundaries and take care of myself when others do things I don't want to do. I can become more self-reliant and depend on myself.

☼ **I can stand firm with what I believe.**

When I think everyone else thinks one way and I don't agree, I am tempted to go along with the crowd. But I don't feel good doing that because I'm not being true to myself. I'm pretending to be someone else just so I can fit in.

But sometimes I am wrong in what I assume others are thinking. Sometimes there are even others who think as I do, but they are just afraid to speak up. When I say what I think, I let them know they aren't alone. And when I speak up nicely but firmly, I let others know my opinion needs to be respected.

Sometimes I am with others who do or say something I don't feel comfortable about. Here is one time I spoke up (or here is one time I could have spoken up and this is the good that might have happened): Solve a problem by taking it over.

I can't change natural talents to please others.

I admire you because I feel safe with you.

_____

_____

_____

_____

The Gaps of Give and Take

How do we differ? Where do you stand on the line?

1. Mark an **✗** at the point on the line where you feel you fit.
2. Mark a **✔** on what other people expect of you.
3. Draw a line between the **✗**, where you are, and the **✔**, others' expectations of you.

I Prefer/I Feel = ✗   **Others Expect = ✔**

What's your comfort zone?

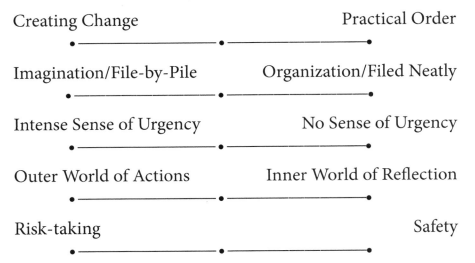

Creating Change   Practical Order

Imagination/File-by-Pile   Organization/Filed Neatly

Intense Sense of Urgency   No Sense of Urgency

Outer World of Actions   Inner World of Reflection

Risk-taking   Safety

The length of the line between the **✗** and the **✔** shows how much other's expectations can differ from what we do or feel comfortable doing.

A short line can mean we naturally fit well with what others expect. But it can also mean we are afraid of being different. A long line can mean we are just different from others. Or it can mean we are rebellious and go "the other way" to stand apart.

Change the way you think about the world

Now I can understand myself and others. I know how I like to do things and how we all fit together in the Friendly Universe.

Change is okay, too, when I understand myself. When we know all the troubles and name them, we're brave. We'll know all the monsters inside. They come from the fear that all of us have, though we're different about them outside. Like when we're afraid that we'll never feel loved, or we fear that we're misunderstood, or we're feeling rejected, alone and neglected, or mixed up on "could", "would" and "should". We know that the four special selves will be there to help and to teach that inside is a light and a love of what's right, and with that we can truly be free.

Bringing the Friendly Universe down to earth includes you and it includes me. It nourishes and encourages us. Order, freedom, understanding, and harmony encircle everyone and hold us all together. Ideas are thrilling. Each discovery is the nature of human ingenuity and leads to new explorations.

And it continues on and on...

"The trees in the street are old trees
used to living with people,
family trees that remember
your grandfather's name."

— *Anonymous Child*

We Are All Different Trees

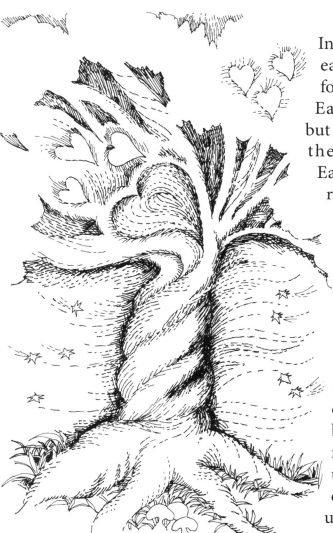

In a synergy forest, each tree reaches for light and grows. Each is different, but each is part of the great forest. Each does its part, reaching for the light of higher understanding.

Old roots and new rules guide us in learning how to work together. Growing from our deep roots—being true to our nature—while understanding others around us, brings joy.

Friendly Universe Collection #1

The Talkabout Chimp Inspires Ideas

Talkabout Chimps love new ideas. They prefer hunches over logic and are called "auditory" people because they respond to tone of voice and like to hear how ideas sound. They like warm, bright colors and bold combinations.

The Talkabout Chimp Is the Dream Mover

Talkabouts communicate things — ideas, creations, inspirations, and questions. ☼ They like to talk about their ideas so others will respond. They love to be inspired. ☼ They like to learn on their own, question the rules, take risks, and try new things. ☼ They are messy people. They file by pile. ☼ They want to be understood and understand why people believe and act as they do. ☼ They are creative problem-solvers; they like to do things a new way. ☼ They look on the bright side, their glass is half full, (not half empty). ☼ When Talkabouts are excited, angry, or loving, everyone within earshot knows. ☼ Feeling they're not understood can cause them stress. ☼ They can be resentful, worried, depressed, and not follow through on commitments.

154   Friendly Universe Collection #1

The Thinkabout Owl
Practices Carefully

Thinkabout Owls love to serve people. They prefer facts to hunches and are called organized people because they take the logical approach to things. Sometimes Thinkabout Owls prefer gray or other light, soft, natural colors, as well as earth tones.

The Thinkabout Owl
Is the Earth Keeper

Thinkabouts take things in as information, rules, data, past experiences. ☼ They are comfortable asking questions, listening, and watching others. ☼ They prefer to gather information and think about it in careful, factual ways. ☼ They find patterns in nature and things to help them create order. That's why Thinkabouts are neat people who put everything back in the right place. ☼ Thinkabouts need time to think things over and make decisions. ☼ They work to keep the world a safe place where things will stay the same because they see the natural patterns in life. ☼ They always see the risks of change; that's why their glass is half empty. They ask, "What's missing in this idea?" ☼ They like things done the right way. ☼ They have feelings and fears, though they rarely put them into words. ☼ They are stressed when there is no order or stability. ☼ They can become negative, unfriendly, and stubborn to get things to go in their particular "right way."

The Lookabout Lion
Leads Tomorrow

Lookabout Lions love knowledge. They prefer to think more than feel. They are called "visual" people because they prefer to look around and picture things in their minds. Lookabout Lions prefer bold, vivid primary colors.

The Lookabout Lion
Sees Vision-Logic

Lookabouts activate things — plans, leadership, authority, and results. ☼ Lookabouts are comfortable answering questions, talking, and expressing themselves. ☼ They see how everything could be made better. ☼ They like to do things their own way. They can envision a plan and explain it very convincingly. They take control of the best ideas and facts and get results. ☼ They own the glass. They like to get to the point; they are willing to take risks and make decisions quickly. ☼ They are both neat and messy people. They keep a lot of things stuffed in their drawers. ☼ They take charge, involve others, and get results. Lack of choice, independence, or vision may cause them stress. ☼ They can be hostile and bossy, yelling to get their own way or show others the highway.

The Feelabout Koala
Tugs Hearts

Feelabout Koalas love action. They prefer to feel more than think. They are called "kinesthetic" people, which means they are sensitive to how their emotions and bodies feel. They prefer warm, soft, quiet, pastel colors. Feelabout Koalas take the journey of the heart.

The Feelabout Koala
Is the Peace Maker

Feelabouts understand such things as feelings=emotions, movement, and impressions. They are friendly people, good at coordinating gatherings because they are cheerful and like to bond, doing things in harmony. ☼ They are adaptive and flexible; they don't like to disagree because they feel caught in the middle of both sides. ☼ To them the glass is both half-full and half-empty. ☼ They want to know the concerns of the group and to be helpful, a part of things. ☼ They are clever at making things by hand and learn by doing. ☼ They like to make things up as they go. ☼ They are both messy and neat people who save up a lot of memorabilia. ☼ They may hold anger and worries inside rather than speak up and risk a quarrel. Lack of harmony or a sense of not belonging may cause them stress. ☼ They can be whiny, gossipy, thin-skinned, or sneaky in order to get their own way. ☼ Being left out or alone is the worst for these nurturers.

Relating to Others

On the next page, pretend you are looking down at the top of a family tree, stretching from its four live clusters.

It's growing from four root values—just as we are doing—with the rings of life compressed within its trunk (the heart of our spirit core).

Find your strongest root value and write your name among the leaves growing there. Next, think about the people you live with — your family and friends.

Put each one's name among the group of leaves growing from the root value you think is the most real and true for that person—**order, freedom, understanding, harmony**.

Next, draw branches connecting your name to each of the other names. Draw thick strong branches to the people you feel close to — those who listen to and understand you the most.

Draw thinner, weaker branches to those who don't relate to you very well. Draw broken branches toward those with whom you have trouble.

Growing
Parts of You

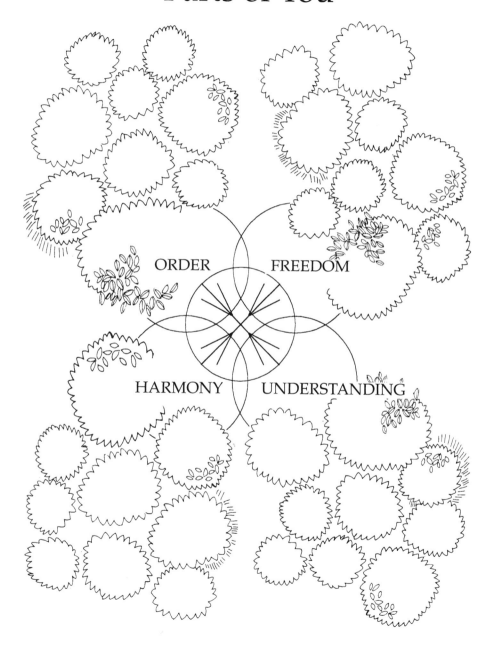

ORDER FREEDOM

HARMONY UNDERSTANDING

You've just drawn your tree of life. Do you see how connected you are? All of those people are part of your life.

Where the connections are weak—where the branches are thin or broken—are relationships that could use some understanding. Think about those people in terms of our Synergy Pals. What might they need from you to make the connection stronger? What can you do to strengthen your growing tree? Look in the section "Smarter Together" for ideas. Human nature is our earthly religion.

Be who you are and say what you feel,
because those who mind don't matter
and those who matter don't mind.

— Dr. Seuss

In many ways the saying "know thyself"
is not well said. It were more practical to say
'Know Other People!"

— Meander, Greek Poet 343-292 BC

I keep six honest serving men
(They taught me all I knew);
Their names are What and Why and When
And How and Where and Who.

— Rudyard Kipling

Your
Thoughtfulness
is a
Work of Heart

LookaboutLion, Talkabout Chimp, Feelabout Koala, and Thinkabout Owl all name their troubles and tell themselves, "Now I'll learn from the rest and be my best when I am part of the whole."

Thinkabout Owl, Lookabout Lion, Talkabout Chimp, and Feelabout Koala learn how to stay healthy and have fun through all of the work and the play, one and all, every day. Each is a part of the whole.

Did you see a little bit of all the Thinkabout, Lookabout, Talkabout, Feelabout parts in yourself — the parts close to your heart? Have you ever wondered why some groups of people work well together and others don't? Some have "Synergy Sense." When your senses of thinking, looking, talking, and feeling work together to solve problems in a balanced way, they are truly your whole brain Synergy Pals.

Glossary
Resource Words for Adults

Bold words *have their own entry.*

Adaptive—One's ability to adjust to circumstances; how the Synergy Pals work collaboratively as a team to find appropriate methods to tackle problems.

Affiliate—The need people have to associate with one another. In synergistic terms, learning to work harmoniously as a team, balancing tolerances and biases.

Anchor—A stimulus arising from experience that, when applied, elicits a specific response: pain or pleasure.

Anxiety—Vague apprehension or fear about the future.

Auditory—Using one's ears as the primary way to perceive the world and access information.

Away From—A tendency to move in a reverse direction, away from someone or something perceived as bringing pain.

Belief—A general expectation or assumption about the way the world operates or other people behave. Beliefs are usually based on one's experience, temperament, and values. Beliefs are learned and can be unlearned or changed.

Chimp, Talkabout—Auditory pal who needs lots of "room" for ideas and creativity; who needs to share and discuss with others, whose opinions they value; and who needs to feel understood on a deep level. Enjoys shaking things up a bit, possibly out of boredom or for shock value. Enthusiast needs follow-through pals. See **Explorer** and **Planner**.

Common Ground—A shared bond, value, belief, experience, need, personality trait, or feeling about a certain situation between two or more people that gives them a feeling of connection on some level personally.

Communication—Exchanging information using verbal or written language and/or various behavioral signals.

Content—The subject matter of life events and/or interactions with others, around which **process** happens.

Decision—Judgment on how best to move away from pain and towards pleasure.

Detailer—A person with a natural talent for noticing, appreciating, planning for, and executing small but often extremely important details. Perfectionist who, given high standards, needs to finish what is started.

Digital—Using language as the primary way to perceive the world and access information.

Disassociation—Retaining a memory without being connected to the feelings associated with the remembered experience.

Dream Mover—Someone who talks about fun and inspired ways to do things. See **Chimp**, **Talkabout** and **Explorer** and **Planner**.

Ecology—The study of how the individual affects the whole, the whole affects the individual, and the total relationship between an individual and his or her external environment. Internal ecology is concerned with the relationships among one's own values, beliefs, expectations, and behavior as one moves toward his or her unlimited potential.

Explorer—A person whose natural talents enable him or her to think out and consider new and different ways of accomplishing things.

Extrovert—One whose behavior is oriented more in an outward direction, toward other people and external circumstances.

Freedom (Rhythms)—The space and lack of restrictions to make choices, conventional or innovative; to think up and explore new and diverse ideas; and to be boldly creative, without offending others. Also, the space and opportunity to express oneself.

Gestalt—The whole picture; the breadth and depth of whatever surrounds one's (usually narrower) focus. When one can see the whole, the detail can be kept in perspective.

Harmony (Rhythms)—The peaceful coexistence of everyone concerned. It is not necessary for everybody to agree on every little thing for harmony to exist; however, it is absolutely necessary for each person to respect the opinions, feelings, ideas, needs, space, and values of everyone else involved.

Inertia—A tendency to remain in a given state, one's comfort zone, resulting in lack of challenge and growth.

Introvert—One whose behavior is oriented more in an inward direction, toward internal conditions.

Kinesthetic—Using one's emotional or tactile senses as the primary ways to perceive the world and access information.

Koala, Feelabout—A kinesthetic pal who needs harmony, connection, empathy, touching (hugs), and personal contact with friends and loved ones. Feelabout Koala needs to have a secure sense of belonging. Retreats to avoid conflict. His or her own feelings and those of others, are major motivators. See **Nurturer**.

Language—There are two levels of language: one's accustomed verbal means of communication (speaking and hearing words), and different individual "thinking languages"—- internal/mental communication, which may be visual, auditory, kinesthetic, or analytical.

Learning Style—An individual's preferred means of acquiring and remembering new information (see **Auditory**, **Digital**, **Kinesthetic**, and **Visual**).

Lion, Lookabout—A big-picture pal who needs options and choices, as well as challenges, and is driven to get results; a visionary, and free spirit. See **Planner** and **Explorer**.

Map—See **Paradigm**.

Matcher/Matching—Comparing input with known information to determine if it is harmonious or not.

Metaphor—A story that conveys a deeper meaning, symbolizing how something works or what it means. The "Synergy Tree" story is a metaphor.

Nurturer—A person with a natural talent for soothing and encouraging others.

Order (Rhythms)—The sense of calm that may result from having a place for everything and everything in its place. Having a schedule or rhythm to one's day or a particular project.

Owl, Thinkabout—A pal who looks at the facts of a project or situation; who needs to feel safe and is most comfortable when things are done in an orderly fashion, in an environment where everything is in its place. One who notices, as well as provides, details. See **Detailer**.

Paradigm—A map, framework, or pattern on which to base a belief system. For example, the world was once thought to be flat and then known to be round: the change in thinking about the shape of the world was a "paradigm shift"

Part—A portion of one's personality — the "parts" of Thinkabout Owl, Talkabout Chimp, Feelabout Koala, and Lookabout Lion within each individual.

Peace Maker—Someone who negotiates an easier way for people to do things. See **Koala**, **Feelabout** and **Nurturer**.

Planner—A person whose natural talents allow him or her to be prepared for opportunities that may develop in a given situation; he or she deals with them efficiently, rather then being surprised and/or totally defeated.

Process—The growing, changing, evolving steps that develop around the content of events and interactions with others.

Rapport—The sense of trust, compatibility, and harmony felt between people.

Rebellion— A form of adolescent behavior designed to purge the mind of its continuing dependence on mother and father. It is characterized by acts intended to anger and disappoint the parents.

Relativistic thinking—The ability to conceptualize issues from diverse perspectives, various points of view, or different frames of reference. Its emergence signals the onset of youth.

Representational Systems—The five senses (sight, sound [hearing and words], smell, touch, taste) used to convey information to the brain.

Rhythm—Core value within a temperament. See **Freedom, Harmony, Order,** and **Understanding**.

Self Actualizing—The act of developing a psychological ability within one's own mind—first through understanding a newly emerging ability and then through granting oneself permission to develop the ability. Achieving the capacity to self-actualize enables one to become self-developing and obviates the need for outside actualizers.

Skill Master—Someone who considers the correct way to do things and likes follow-through. See **Owl, Thinkabout** and **Detailer**.

State—The status and sum total of what one thinks, feels, and does at any given time. How emotions are managed may depend upon the given circumstances.

Synergy—The result of interactions of heterogeneous parts multipying the effect of the whole. The whole equals more than the sum of the parts. The interrelatedness of life; people are unique, yet more alike than different, and we are all creatively connected in some way.

Temperament—One's natural behavior or method of action, based on personality. A Synergy Pal, for example, may behave primarily as a **Thinkabout Owl** but also have **Talkabout Chimp**, **Lookabout Lion**, and **Feelabout Koala** aspects to his or her personality and behavior; order, understanding, freedom, harmony are anthropomorphic values or metaphors for consistently driven behaviors.

Toward—A preference to move closer to pleasure associated with someone or something.

Unconscious functioning—Psychological activity that occurs outside of awareness.

Understanding (Rhythms)—The ability to not only listen to someone, but to also comprehend what is being said. Empathizing rather than just sympathizing with a loved one's pain (given that friends are loved ones); the capacity to feel, not just observe.

Value—One's individual (or a group's) priorities, against which people and events are measured for worthiness; for instance, **Order**, **Freedom**, **Understanding**, and **Harmony** are values, that, if denied, cause suffering.

Vision Leader—Someone who seeks for a new way to do things. See **Lion**, **Lookabout** and **Explorer/Planner**.

Visual—Using one's eyes as the primary way to perceive the world and access information.

Youth—the stage of life that follows adolescence and is characterized by the ability to think relativistically.

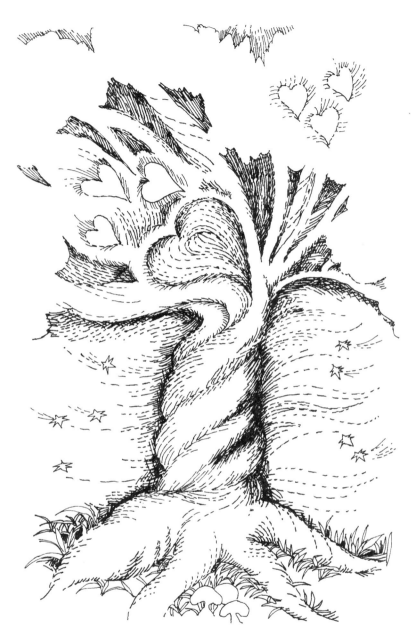

Wisdom is the tree of life to those
who embrace her; those who lay
hold of her will be blessed.

Proverbs 3.18 NIV

Recommended Reading

Armstrong, Thomas, PhD, *You're Smarter Than You Think: A Kid's Guide to Multiple Intelligences*. Free Spirit Publishing, 2003.

Bandler, Richard, Grinder, John, and Satir, Virginia, *Changing With Families*. Science and Behavior Books, 1976.

Bridges, William, *Managing Transitions: Making the Most of Change*. Da Capo Lifelong, 2009.

Buckingham Marcus and Clifton, Donald O., *Now Discover Your Strengths*. Free Press, 2001.

Burnham, Terry and Phelan, Jay, *Mean Genes*. Perseus Publishing, 2000.

Campbell, Joseph, *The Hero's Journey*. Harper & Row, 1990.

Carey, William B., *Understanding Your Child's Temperament*. Macmillan, 2005, 1997.

Gardner, Howard, *Five Minds for the Future*, Harvard Business Press, 2008.

Gladwell, Malcolm, *The Outliers: the Story of Success*. Little, Brown and Company, 2008.

Goleman, Daniel, *Emotional Intelligence*. Bantam Books, 1995.

Grandin, Temple, and Duffy, Kate, *Developing Talents: Careers for Individuals with Asperger Syndrome and High-Functioning Autism*. Shawnee Mission, KS: Autism Asperger Pub. Co., 2008.

Hartmann, Thomas, *Focus Your Energies*. Mythical Intelligence, 1994.

Gordon, Gary, *Building Engaged Schools: Getting the Most out of America's Classrooms*. The Gallup Organization, 2006.

Johansson, Frans, *Medici Effect: Breakthrough Insights at the Intersection of Ideas, Concepts & Cultures*. Harvard Business School Publishing, 2004.

Jung, Carl, *Psychological Types*. Pantheon, 1953.

Kandel, Eric R., *In Search of Memory: The Emergence of the New Science of Mind*. WW. Norton Company, 2006.

Keirsey, David, and Bates, Marilyn, *Please Understand Me: An Essay on Temperament Styles*. Prometheus Nemesis, 1978.

Kristal, Jan, *The Temperament Perspective: Working With Children's Behavioral Styles*. Brookes Publishing Co., 2005.

Lankton, Stephen R., *Practical Magic: The Clinical Applications of Neuro-Linguistic Programming*. Meta Publications, 1979.

Levine, Mel, *A Mind at a Time*. Simon & Schuster, 2002.

Levitin, Daniel J., *The World in Six Songs*. Penguin Group, 2008.

Myers, Isabel Briggs with Peter B. Myers, *Gifts Differing: Understanding Personality Type*. Consulting Psychologists Press, 1995.

Neville, Helen and Diane Clark Johnson, *Temperament Tools: Working With Your Child's Inborn Traits*. Parenting Press, 1998.

Pink, Daniel H., *A Whole New Mind: Why Right-brainers Will Rule the Future*. Riverhead Books, 2005.

Pollan, Michael, *The Botany of Desire: A Plant's-Eye View of the World*. New York: Random House, 2002.

Reverman, Ardys, *In the Creative Circle*. Taproots Press, 1993.

Reverman, Ardys, *Teamwork is Child's Play*. Taproots Press, 1995.

Reverman, Ardys, *Team Smart SQ: Redefining What It Means to Be Smart*. Friendly Universe Collections, 2006.

Reverman, Ardys, *heart2heart: Be Yourself — Everone Else Is Taken*. Friendly Universe Collections, 2011.

Reverman, Ardys, *Turning Points, Journey to Self Discovery*. Friendly Universe Collections, 2011.

Reverman, Ardys, *Treasure Quest, We Are Connected*. Friendly Universe Collections, 2011.

Robbins, Anthony, *Unlimited Power*. Simon and Schuster, 1986.

Robinson, Ken, Ph.D., *The Element: How finding Your Passion Changes Everything*. Viking, 2009.

Rosen, Sidney, *My Voice Will Go with You: The Teaching Tales of Milton H. Erickson, M.D.*. New York: Norton, 1982.

Rosenberg, Marshall B., Ph.D., *Nonviolent Communication, A Language of Life*. Puddle Dancer Press, 2003.

Russell, Peter, *The Global Brain*. J.P. Tarcher, 1983.

Satir, Virginia, *Your Many Faces: First Step to Being Loved*. CLArts, 1978.

Schiller Pam and Phipps Pat, *Starting with Stories: Engaging Multiple Intelligences*. Gryphon House, 2006.

Shaywitz, Sally, M.D., *Overcoming Dyslexia: a New and Complete Science-based Program for Reading Problems at Any Level*. Alfred A. Knoft, 2003.

Sloat, Donald E., PhD., *The Dangers of Growing Up in a Christian Home*. Thomas, Nelson Publishers, 1986.

Smith, Lendon H., *Hyper Kids*. Shaw/Spelling, 1990.

Strauss, William and Howe, Neil, *The Fourth Turning*. Broadway Books, 1997.

Tieger, Paul D. and Barbara Barron-Tieger, *Do What You Are*. Little Brown & Co., 1992.

Wiseman Rosalind, *Queen Bees and Wannabees*. Three Rivers Press, 2002.

Wood, Tracey, *Overcoming Dyslexia for Dummies*. Wiley Publishing, Inc., 2006.

Did you know that everybody is good at something? When we make our differences work together, that's heart2heart, a game of self-discovery.

A new way of whole-brain learning for the 21st century: heart2heart game for the family and classroom.
Please order heart2heart today!

http://gifts.barnesandnoble.com/Toys-games/
Heart-To-Heart-Game/e/183338000499

Usually ships within 24 hours • UPC: 183338000499

http://www.amazon.com/Discovery-Bay-Games-1049-
Heart/dp/097918276X/ref=sr_1_12?ie=UTF8&s=toys-and-
games&qid=1280280529&sr=1-12

www.friendlyuniverse.com

Discover How Your Child's Special Gifts Fit Well With Others

THE FRIENDLY UNIVERSE
C O L L E C T I O N

ISBN 0-9625385-6-6

ISBN 0-9625385-7-4

ISBN 0-9625385-8-2

ISBN 0-9625385-0-6

Find out with this New SQ Personality Quiz

Ardys Reverman, Ph.D., is internationally acclaimed as an innovative educator on the marvels and mysteries of the brain. Originally inspired by her own life as a Mom, her quest to understand innate talents add up to different ways of being smarter together. To learn more about her work and books go to: www.friendlyuniverse.com

For UG/Grad Course Registration Information www.friendlyuniverse.com

• SQ is not IQ — the latest brain science reveals, and research confirms, the importance of our synergy quotient.
• It's rewarding to discover your child's strengths — the earlier the better.
• All children learn differently, yet we tend to treat them as if they are the same.
• Help your child to understand and connect with others.
• We are all part of something larger than ourselves.
• Be smarter together for success in an uncertain world.
• A must read and DO to understand your personality.

These are wonderful Books that show you how to better understand and bring out the best in you and those who matter most in your life. The poems, illustrations and insights are powerful.

Brian Tracy, Ph.D.
author of No Excuses -The Power of Self Discipline

Ardys Reverman PhD

drardy@friendlyuniverse.com www.friendlyuniverse.com
or www.synergypals.com

Newly updated and revised editions available as a set

Acknowledgments

My Own Family Tree

Every tree needs good soil for deep taproots, so it can receive the nourishment that gives it the supple strength to bend and grow. To all, I express my love and appreciation. This book grew from the roots of those who matter most to me: my kin, friends, and a whole lot of talented minds recognizing our tree is life. Imagine a Friendly Universe within and without that reflects nature's secret to give back with our talents. From ancient times to today, brave and curious souls have evolved our thinking, with many fields of study converging to create our world. The future belongs to those who, in their own way and by being themselves, find their place where talent and desire come together. They give back more than they know by living an ordinary life and making it extraordinary.

Whether we knew it or not at the time, my children Peter, Alex and Liza inspired this book. Son-in-law Gabe and daughter-in-law Kerry show me the deeply rooted bonds of kinship. I continue to love and learn from the intuitive support of my Mama, Papa, my beloved late husband Jack, and brothers Eldon, Oliver and Stanley. My grandchildren are showing me anew each child's full circle of unique talents. Caroline, Eloise, Anna, Amelia, Ella, Alex Jr., and Cash are beautiful reminders that the miracle of life starts inside another human being; this is how we are made to interact with each other. This work is my best attempt to capture the spirit and practice of what we all strive for every day, discovering the things we love to do and the things we are good at in order to give back. Together we are on an adventure of forgiveness as we learn how to best love one another. Thanks everyone for the reality checks.

This work is also grounded in my belief that all problems have solutions, a strong belief I inherited from my first role models. My heartfelt thanks to my parents who intuitively defined the concept of right relationship; living one's own life with purpose and passion. Against all temperament odds my parents learned to make a good fit intuitively through love and laughter. My beloved mother, Ella Meissner Hellmann, an immigrant gifted with visual hope and determination, became a builder. My intuitive father, Edward Charles Urbigkeit, expressed his kinesthetic empathy for others through his genius for music. Awareness of differentiated learning was unknown in the polarized twentieth century, a time of rigid religious, social, cultural and gender beliefs. Little was known about how a child learns. Understanding temperaments helped open a treasure map revealing a new awareness of each other's emotional needs and wants. Do unto others what they would have you do unto them.

Mother nature is cunning and always imposing a new problem, reminding us that the brain feeds itself by learning. Meanwhile our animal spirits are loose. Both fast and flexible, the synergy pals remind us to discover our gifts to give something back from the investment of our energy and our own self-worth. Be who you are and love everything. Do what your talent dictates. Give children their own empowerment to achieve from their own success. The tension of embodying opposites co-create and co-evolve us in relationship.

Thank you, all who confidently fine-tuned the end product. I am grateful to the late Charlotte Lewis, who made my dream pictures come true. Many others thoughtfully organized a body of information. Joan Pinkert edited, laid out text, and tailored designs to my specifications; Marion Dansky of "Nanimals" created Synergy Pals puppet prototypes; Richard Ferguson of Ferguson Fine Arts developed the cover design; my good neighbor Patty Fale contributed photography; and Helen Rockey inspired my heart2heart game adventure. Without you there's no…US.

This is how my book grew; this is how I grow. To make the tree whole, we have to know where the branches are broken. Creativity, courage and insight strengthen the broken places of each tree growing from root to branches.

love and laughter,

Trudy

Index